HOCKEY

THOMAS S. OWENS
DIANA STAR HELMER

TWENTY-FIRST CENTURY BOOKS

BROOKFIELD, CONNECTICUT

To you, hockey's future.
Shoot for your goal!

Cover photograph courtesy of Allsport (© Craig Melvin)

Photographs courtesy of Allsport: pp. 6 (© Tim Brokema), 9 (© Elsa Hasch), 16 (© Harry Scull), 17 (© Harry Scull), 20 (© Doug Pensinger), 22 (© Rick Stewart), 24 (© Craig Jones), 44 (© Rick Stewart), 52 (© Robert Laberge), 54 (© Robert Laberge); AP/Wide World Photos: pp. 12, 14; Hockey Hall of Fame: pp. 13 (© Dave Sandford), 27 (© Graphic Artists), 47 left (© Imperial Oil-Turofsky); Bruce Bennett Studios: pp. 15 (© M. DiGirolamo), 28 (© R. Laberge), 32 (© J. Leary), 38 (© M. DiGiacomo), 40 (© Brian Winkler), 47 right (© J. Giamundo), 50 (© J. McIsaac); UPI/Corbis-Bettmann: p. 35

Designed by Molly Heron

Owens, Tom, 1960–
     Hockey / Thomas S. Owens and Diana Star Helmer.
     p. cm. — (Game Plan)
     Includes bibliographical references (p.) and index.
     Summary: Describes how professional hockey teams prepare for games, analyze the games afterwards for improvement, develop strategies, and build themselves through player selection.
     ISBN 0-7613-3236-7 (lib. bdg.)
     1. Hockey—Juvenile literature. [1. Hockey.]
I. Helmer, Diana Star, 1962– . II. Title. III. Series: Owens, Tom, 1960– Game plan.
GV847.25.O94   1999
796.962—dc21   98-40624   CIP
                                                 AC

Published by Twenty-First Century Books
A Division of The Millbrook Press, Inc.
2 Old New Milford Road
Brookfield, Connecticut 06804

CONTENTS

TWO PATHS, ONE GOAL

The Stanley Cup is what players in the National Hockey League (NHL) work for and wait for, through years and careers. When the Detroit Red Wings took home the Cup in 1997, the feeling was like a hundred birthdays, a thousand fireworks, a million people cheering. And the Red Wings had a lifetime to hold that feeling, to know they were champions, to know they were the best.

"A year ago, it was a great day," said Detroit center Kris Draper in 1998, "but that was a long time ago."

The Red Wings enjoyed their unstoppable reputation for six days in 1997. Then, on June 13, 1997, their Stanley Cup seemed to lose some of its shine.

Two players, Slava Fetisov and all-star defenseman Vladimir Konstantinov, had gone golfing with team massage therapist Sergei Mnatsakanov. On the way home, their limousine driver fell asleep at the wheel. The crash into a tree almost killed Konstantinov and Mnatsakanov, leaving both with brain injuries. Forty-year-old Fetisov slowly recovered, but Konstantinov's career was over.

"When you win a championship in a team sport, there is a certain amount of invincibility that you take with you through the off-season," Detroit winger Brendan Shanahan told *USA TODAY*. "Some teams may get complacent. But our celebration was short-lived. We were taught a very valuable lesson."

Throughout the next season, the Red Wings chose a painful game plan: They refused to forget their loss. To remember that their teammate was special, they kept Konstantinov's locker stall untouched, still filled with his gear. Players wore a patch, containing the initials of their two injured friends. In Russian and in English, the patch read: BELIEVE. Their belief took the Red Wings back to the Western Conference finals. If they could beat the Dallas Stars, Detroit would have another chance at the Stanley Cup.

Chris Osgood of the Detroit Red Wings wears a circular "Believe" patch in honor of Vladimir Konstantinov and Sergei Mnatsakanov, who were injured in a June 1997 automobile accident.

PLAYING SHORT-HANDED

The Stars had carved out the top win-loss record among NHL teams in 1997–1998. They ended the regular season with a six-game winning streak. Dallas's defensive game plan was the pressure trap, a new twist on the old idea of moving the whole team like a line of military tanks.

But as the conference neared, Dallas struggled to figure out how to work that plan without center Joe Nieuwendyk, who had scored 37 goals before a knee injury took him out of the playoffs. "He is the key guy on their power play," said Detroit coach Scotty Bowman.

Without their star, the Stars scraped up only 14 shots in the first conference match-up. Still, hopes ran high for Dallas when they kept the first period scoreless. But "We just didn't play the same as we did in the first period," Dallas forward Pat Verbeek told reporters after the game. "We just have to stay with our game plan longer than we did tonight. It really boils down to one-on-one battles," to Stars players getting past their opponents to where they need to be. The Western Conference opener became a 2–0 win for Detroit.

But the Stars burned Detroit goalie Chris Osgood twice in Game 2. First, Osgood misfired a pass into a flock of Stars. Second, Osgood watched a shot trickle past him to the net, its spin slowly bumping over rough ice. Osgood assumed a teammate had blocked the shot. Detroit learned that any game plan depends on team concentration, as Dallas evened the series with a 3–1 win at home.

Offensive fireworks flared in Game 3. Behind 4–0, Dallas fired off shot after shot, 34 in all, finally sinking three goals—in a row! Detroit only took 20 tries that night, but their 5 successful shots meant that the Red

. . . .

What would happen if the NHL settled tied games with shoot-outs? When tied, teams get a five-minute sudden-death overtime. If no one scores, each team chooses five players. Each gets a penalty shot after bringing up the puck from center ice. The team making the most penalty goals wins. Another tie means another shoot-out. That's how Sweden won the gold medal against Canada in the 1994 Olympics.

Wings led the series, two games to one. Even so, Dallas was reminded of a vital, simple strategy: More shots equal more scoring chances.

A 3–2 Detroit victory in Game 4 inched Dallas to the edge of post-season elimination. At the 11:30 mark in the third period, Steve Yzerman seized a loose puck, starting the crucial score while Dallas was distracted making a lineup change. Vyacheslav Kozlov blew a shot over the right shoulder of Stars goalie Ed Belfour, all because Dallas forgot one of the oldest, easiest strategies: Keep your eye on the puck.

MAKING A COMEBACK

The roar coming after this crucial point was nothing, however, compared with the deafening sounds of the Detroit crowd during a first pe-riod timeout. That was when the public-address system had blared that Konstantinov and Mnat-sakanov were watching the game from the private suite of Detroit owner Mike Ilitch. The former star player was attending his first Red Wings home game since the accident the previous year. A sellout crowd of 19,983 thundered its gratitude and appreciation for 95 endless, over-powering seconds.

> . . . .
>
> **An NHL game lasts for three 20-minute periods. In a 1936 playoff, Detroit needed six overtime periods to beat Montreal, 1–0. Teams were on the ice for nearly three hours.**

Back in Texas for Game 5, the Stars still did not revive. With only 85 seconds left, Detroit led 2–1. Guy Carbonneau had a chance to tie the game—until he was upended. He tried again—and went down again. With only seconds left, Carbonneau took still another shot, and this time sent the game into overtime.

It didn't last long. Just 46 seconds into overtime, Stars forward Jamie Langenbrunner squirted a bouncing 70-foot shot past goalie Osgood. Detroit captain Yzerman didn't blame Osgood. "It wasn't a bad goal. It was a fluky goal," he said. A literal long shot—70 feet! But Osgood learned yet again that the simplest strategies win games. Osgood for-got to expect the unexpected. Dallas didn't, and their 3–2 triumph sparked a glimmer of hope in the Dallas sky.

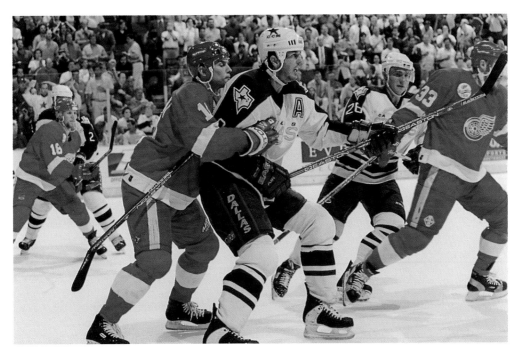

Action in Game 5 of the 1998 Western Conference Finals shows Red Wings Steve Yzerman trying to stop Stars Mike Modano.

For the traditional handshake at center ice after Game 5, Osgood remembered an equally important strategy: moving past the past and concentrating on the game at hand with good humor. Shaking hands with Stars shooter Langenbrunner, Osgood reported, "I said, 'We made it go another.' He got a chuckle out of that."

Osgood wouldn't provide any more laughs for Dallas. He would post a 2–0 shutout to redeem himself in Game 6. Defenseman Larry Murphy would continue Detroit's demonstration of technique. Substituting quickly as Bob Rouse hustled off the ice, Murphy went almost undetected, getting open for a backhanded goal at the 6:20 mark in the first period. Not only did Murphy get a jump on the play with his heads-

> **What is in a name?** "Roller hockey" once was a game played on roller skates. Now, "in-line hockey" is the same game with in-line skates. "Street hockey" is a simple game played in shoes with no wheels. More than 250,000 boys and girls play in leagues featuring these off-ice cousins of the sport.

up entry into the game, but he used a type of shot that kept the goal guardian off guard. "I didn't know if I had time to come across to my forehand. With a backhand shot, it's tough to read how the shot (puck) comes off the blade. It's tough for any goaltender."

When scoring first, the Red Wings would boast a 9–1 record through the first three rounds of the playoff.

In those last six games against the Stars, the Red Wings won the battle of numbers, even when outnumbered. In penalty-killing situations, Detroit shut down Dallas in 29 of 30 tries. For though the Stars had led the league in power-play production during the regular season, Dallas seemed lost in power-play chances without Nieuwendyk.

The Red Wings' game plan was simpler. Teamwork, the act of spreading out the workload and the worry, would be Detroit's return ticket to a second-straight Stanley Cup battle.

THE BRAINS BEHIND THE GAMES

2

A team's game plan starts before the first puck hits the ice. Before the planners can decide how to win, they need to decide who will try to do the winning.

Choosing a hockey team takes a team effort. Many minds play a part in picking players for the upcoming season: Owners, coaches, general managers, and scouts all try to agree on what will be best for the team's future. The planning goes on all through the year.

For example, as Dallas neared the 1998 playoffs, the team considered how to guarantee a postseason spot. That's why the Stars gave up young talent in Todd Harvey, trading him to the New York Rangers for veterans Brian Skrudland and Mike Keane. By the time of the trade, the Rangers knew they had little hope of a playoff spot. They wanted to dump the huge, multiyear contracts of free-agents Skrudland and Keane. Money matters: The Rangers could pay Harvey less. However, the patience of team officials mattered most: Newcomer Harvey would be able to aid the team for seasons to come.

CAN HAPPINESS BE BOUGHT?

For the Stars, the future was now. "I'm not a talent evaluator," said Dallas president Jim Lites. "I know my role, and I trust my hockey people." One of those "hockey people" was general manager Bob Gainey, a player for 16 years and former Montreal Canadiens team captain. After his playing days, Gainey turned head coach, then general manager. Lites's trust in Gainey's judgment had paid off earlier that season, when center Mike Modano signed a six-year $43.5 million contract to kick off the 1997–1998 post-season. "That's half the amount I spent to buy the team," team owner Tom Hicks had told reporters. However, Modano's star power gave more than team leadership. Modano's popularity meant that the Stars sold more tickets, allowing the team to build a new arena for the year 2000.

That same year, the Detroit Red Wings didn't know if they wanted to win at any cost. They considered saying good-bye to Sergei Fedorov, the star center who had played out his existing contract following the Red Wings' 1997 Stanley Cup championship. Fedorov could sign with another team only if that team paid more than Detroit. Waiting for a good offer, Fedorov sat out the first 59 games of the season. Finally, the Carolina Hurricanes bid on Fedorov, offering him a $12 million bonus if

On April 13, 1998, Dallas Stars owner Tom Hicks (*left*), all-star Mike Modano (*center*), and team general manager Bob Gainey (*right*) announced Modano's $43.5 million contract.

the team reached the Western Conference finals. (Carolina, never a sure thing for the postseason, may not have been risking a lot with such a promise!) But by this time, Fedorov's old team had a very real chance at a repeat championship. Detroit decided to keep their star by matching Carolina's offer—including the $12 million. Fedorov played his first game that year on February 27.

Keeping good players such as Detroit Red Wings center Sergei Fedorov can be costly to a team, but the cost is all part of forming a winning game plan.

BARK, BITE, OR BOND

Building a team is a never-ending process. Players are continually acquired and let go, and continually learning new ways to help their team. How do coaches get players to do what needs to be done?

Red Wings coach Scotty Bowman barks and growls, giving players a strict teacher as leader. "He keeps all the players on edge," Detroit defenseman Bob Rouse told *USA TODAY*. "You never are certain what to expect from him, and I think that's one of the reasons why he is so successful. He's been hard on every player in this room at one time or another. Players know they will be in his doghouse at one time or another. How players react to that will determine how well [they] do."

Detroit coach Scotty Bowman gives hand-signal instructions from the bench during Game 2 of the 1998 Stanley Cup Finals.

Barry Smith, Detroit's assistant coach, says Bowman's barking manner gives players something to sink their teeth into. "He teaches things that make you a winner," Smith said. "You learn details [such as] the defensive side of the puck, don't cheat the game, play hard both ways, short shifts, a team mentality, and those kind of things. Those things will help you win, because that takes care of almost all situations."

Bowman's barking chased the Red Wings into the playoffs. Their opponents, the Capitals, got there more quietly. Ron Wilson, the first-year head coach of the Washington Capitals, used positive reinforcement to get players excited. One of his tactics was a "Countdown to the

Cup" board inside the locker room. A number, starting with 16, was posted. Wilson knew that the players knew 16 was the magic number of wins the future championship team needed through four rounds of postseason play. After each win, the team would choose a star to tear the old number off the wall. The media gave Wilson rave reviews for his cheerleading style.

But whether a coach chooses to bark at or bond with his players, nearly all hire "video coordinators" to help them make their points. Video coordinators shoot and maintain videotapes of games and practices, along with acquiring videos of other teams. Coaches can tell and *show* players things they are doing right or wrong. Seeing is believing. Plus, footage of a tricky move may help a coach teach that move to others—or ways to avoid being beaten by that play.

Recording and video equipment are used to provide behind-the-scenes analysis of games.

BODIES, MINDS AND SPIRITS

A coach's style may indicate a team's style behind the scenes. The Hartford Whalers, before they moved and became the North Carolina Hurricanes, listed a woman employee as a "motivational consultant." Many teams hire psychologists or counselors to help players' attitudes. However, the Florida Panthers want results they can really see: They list a

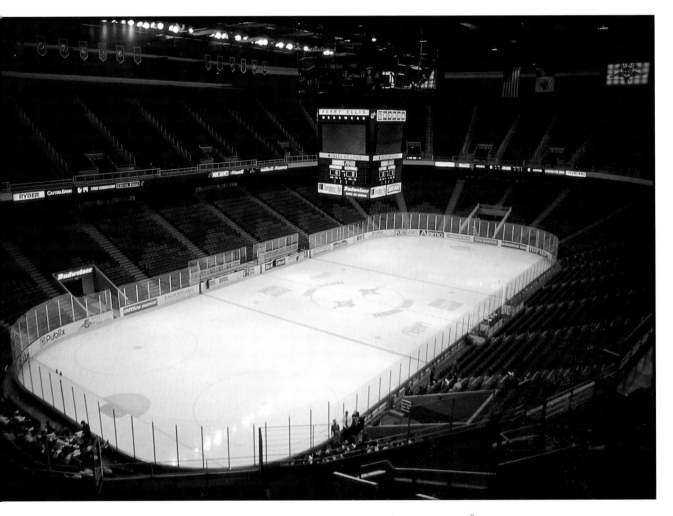

A standard NHL hockey rink measures 200 feet by 85 feet, with rounded corners. There is a goal area at either end, and the space between the goals is divided into three equal zones. At game time, a goal cage is put at each end in the goal area.

The Zamboni ice resurfacer was invented by Frank Zamboni in 1949. The machine shaves the ice, removes the shavings, washes the ice, and applies a final coat of water to provide a new smooth surface.

plastic surgeon in their official directory, a doctor the team keeps to mend the expected facial injuries of players. But most teams rely on more traditional therapies. Massage is a longtime favorite. A masseur, someone who can rub bruised, aching muscles, may keep players on the ice longer. A pregame massage may relax players prone to pulling muscles.

"The trainers and equipment managers are the glue that holds the teams together," said Peter Demers, Los Angeles Kings trainer since 1980. Demers tapes the body parts of many players before games to protect them from extra wear and tear. During games, Demers stays by the bench to aid injured players with stitches for cuts or other quick assistance. When injuries happen, Demers becomes a rehabilitation trainer, helping hurt players to heal and get on the ice again.

Because the right equipment helps athletes play better and avoid injury, some teams like Detroit have the same person serve as both trainer and equipment manager. But, L.A.'s Demers points out, "The game's about the players, not about the trainers." When a player avoids injury, or heals quicker than the doctor thought, the athlete gets the glory—but the training staff could rightfully take credit for an assist.

Who knows what jobs will help a team win? Some clubs even name a "music coordinator." All those exciting rock-and-roll sing-alongs, funny tunes or the now-recorded organ-played cheers are picked to be played at certain times in a game by a person, an expert at reading a game and a crowd. An enthusiastic home crowd can make a difference in a game—ask any player.

Only some of the people on winning teams wear skates. A good game plan requires lots of brains behind the games.

BUILDING A WINNER

On paper, the Red Wings and Capitals seemed destined for the Stanley Cup in 1998. Their strong offensive and defensive stats, their sizes and ages indicated an exciting, unpredictable match. But the differences between the teams started long before the statistics.

In the eyes of many fans, Washington became a winner on March 1, 1997. That day, the Capitals made a shocking trade with the Boston Bruins. Boston sent three big-name players—Adam Oates, Rick Tocchet, and goalie Bill Ranford—in exchange for Washington's Jim Carey (a onetime Vezina Trophy winner as the league's top goalie) and two promising newcomers, Jason Allison and Anson Carter.

How could Boston give up Oates, who had been praised by the hockey media as one of the ten greatest passers ever? Probably because, off the ice, Oates was anything but cool. He didn't like the way the Bruins were being built—and he didn't mind saying so. "They [the Bruins] have a lot of talent. [This trade] is a chance for them now to get to that next level," Oates said after leaving. "But I think the question is going to be that when the team gets a little bit better, and they have to pay these guys [more], what is going to happen? If they want to make a team that is going to compete, they are going to have to pay some guys. If they do, then great. They will have a great team. But if they don't, then they are going to have to turn it around again and do the same thing and constantly upgrade and keep the payroll low. It depends on what their philosophy is. . . . I don't know who really runs the show there, if it is ownership or management."

Boston viewed his attitude, his star's salary, and his 35-year-old body as reasons to look for younger, cheaper help for the future. But Washington was happy with the rebel: Oates played in all 82 regular-season games for the Capitals. "He's played with injuries. He's a warrior," Capitals coach Ron Wilson told *USA TODAY*.

A team may balance its roster by trading players. The Boston Bruins traded Adam Oates, shown here fighting Bryan Smolinski for the puck, to the Washington Capitals in March 1997.

Another key to the Boston/Washington trade was a change in goalies for both teams. Washington saw a bigger change: Their new goalie Ranford was injured in the season opener, and never matched his past fame. However, his substitute, Olaf Kolzig, became more than a decent replacement—his success made him a rising star.

Meanwhile, the Bruins grew so frustrated with onetime star Carey that they finally banished him to the minors as the season ended. Still, Boston got more than it hoped for from center Allison, who played like a polished veteran. He collected 83 points in 81 games (33 goals and 50 assists). With Washington, one of his biggest problems had been a lack of starting time in the Caps' veteran lineup.

CATCHING A GOOD UPDRAFT

Boston's and Washington's woes show why many teams consider trades and free-agent signings quick, *temporary* fixes. Nothing builds a long-term winner better than smart draft picks.

The entry draft makes sure that one rich team doesn't hire all the best amateur players. In a draft, amateurs are gathered together so NHL teams can take turns choosing. It's a lot like kids choosing teams on the playground. When an NHL hopeful is chosen in the draft by a team, only that team has the right to sign the player to a contract. Of course, the draftee can say no to the money offered. However, the player then has to wait until the next year's draft to be chosen by another team.

The order of team selection is determined by the team's regular-season record. Because Dallas won the Presidents' Trophy for the best win-loss mark in 1997, it could not choose until 27th, or last, in the first round the following year. The teams with the poorest records, supposedly needing the most improvement, get the first picks in this nine-round event.

Who can be drafted? According to the NHL, any player wanting to be considered for the draft has to be at least 16 years old, with at least one season of experience in an approved junior or "rated" amateur league. This includes college players and, since the early 1990s, European players.

Teams have looked to the champion Red Wings for team-building hints. Detroit has eight full-time talent scouts, about the same as most other teams. Two cover Canada, two the United States, one scouts the Czech Republic, one directs European scouting, one watches the minor leagues, and one monitors other NHL teams. Of course, all scouts can rely on common information: Independent scouting services write reports shared with many teams. New player information is rarely top-secret, but the details can still be useful and affordable to a small staff of team scouts.

The NHL entry draft is a very important part of building a successful team. An NHL hopeful must be an amateur to be eligible for the entry draft. The 1998 draft took place in Marine Midland Arena in Buffalo, New York.

PICKING ON OTHER TEAMS

All teams participate in the yearly entry draft. But when the NHL expands, adding one or more new teams, an expansion draft is held, and only the new teams pick players.

The Nashville Predators joined the NHL for the 1998–1999 season. An expansion draft allowed the new team to pick one player from the roster of each existing team. But the Predators couldn't pick just anyone: Teams were allowed to put a certain number of players off-limits. The league gave teams two choices of grouping players who could be protected from the draft. A team could guard

Plan A	or	Plan B
9 forwards		7 forwards
5 defensemen		3 defensemen
1 goaltender		2 goaltenders
1 skater		1 skater

From the unprotected players, the NHL expected Nashville to choose 26, one from each team, to make a roster that included

13 forwards
8 defensemen
3 goaltenders

Established teams sweated over which players to protect, knowing that anyone not on the list would be lost if Nashville picked them. In the past, old teams have offered expansion clubs future draft picks or traded players in return for *not* selecting an unprotected team member. But Nashville didn't make deals before the 1998 draft. So the old teams used various game plans in making their protected lists. They tried to

There is no excuse for not protecting your head. When the NHL made helmets a requirement for all players, only players who had signed pro contracts before June 1, 1979, or those signing waivers, were excluded. Essentially, the waiver said, "If I get hurt not wearing a helmet, it is my own fault."

guess: Could Nashville afford to choose star players who had huge contracts? Would the Predators risk choosing players who were recovering from injuries?

In one of the most surprising choices on the protected list, Pittsburgh sheltered Mario Lemieux. Lemieux had retired after the 1996–1997 season. The superstar center had hung up his skates at age 31 to fight a form of cancer called Hodgkin's disease. Yet, he remained under contract with the Penguins. Pittsburgh hadn't given up hope that Lemieux would someday get well and return to the ice. If this local hero made a comeback with another team, other Pen-

> Detroit was famous for car factory "production lines," creating countless automobiles quickly. In 1946 the Red Wings teamed rookie right wing Gordie Howe, Ted Lindsay at left wing, and Sid Abel as center. As the trio (with Alex Delvecchio succeeding Abel) gave the Red Wings a seven-season run with hockey's best win-loss record, Detroit nicknamed the group the "production line."

Mario Lemieux, a superstar with the Pittsburgh Penguins, retired after the 1996-1997 season. Here he acknowledges a goal in one of his final Stanley Cup playoff games.

guins players might be angry. Hurt Pittsburgh fans might buy fewer tickets.

Other teams expected Nashville to leave veteran players alone and choose all the young talent, players who could still be paid less money and might stay with the new team for years to come.

Teams need time and money to stick to a team-building game plan. Most of all, the team builders need patience. Trades and free-agency may let teams buy a onetime title. But the dynasty, the team that wins for years, only comes by letting young players become great together. In time, those winners are more than a team. They are a family.

4 TWO GOOD WINGS

The left and right wings can help a hockey team fly or flounder.

Moving up and down the left and right sides of the ice, the wingers feed passes to the center while rebounding errant shots. Wingers work in tandem to keep a team moving. Like the center, left and right wingers are sometimes called "forwards."

Coach Scotty Bowman put his Detroit wingers at the front of a game plan that became famous. In the "left wing lock defensive system," a left winger and two defensemen lurk near the blue line. Before the opponents can set a play out of their own territory, the right wing and center swoop in from the right. A turnover or icing are likely results, as the left side of the ice is the only escape. The left winger becomes the star roadblock. Bowman's brainstorm gave the wing positions importance, with or without the puck.

In years past, the headline-grabbing wingers have often been ones whose scoring soars. Hockey history places right winger Gordie Howe at the top of most "best" lists. "Mr. Hockey" played 26 seasons in the NHL, scoring 1,846 points. He played his last professional hockey in 1980, at the age of 51. One of Howe's greatest feats was that he could shoot left- or right-handed, like the baseball "switch hitter."

Rivaling Howe as right winger was Maurice "Rocket" Richard. In 18 years, Richard helped earn eight Stanley Cup championships for the Montreal Canadiens. Traditionally, a left-handed shooter like "Rocket" would play the left-side position, because a left-handed swing most naturally travels to the right. But Richard was among the first "opposite" shooters—and quick, unexpected shots are always good offense.

Working together, wingers can form fearsome offensive machines. Just as in basketball's fast break, a winger can shine in a breakaway to the goal by outskating the defensemen. Speed helps—but so do brains.

Gordie Howe played for the Detroit Red Wings from the 1946-1947 season through the 1970-1971 season. He retired from the Hartford Whalers after the 1979-1980 season.

BRAINS AND BRAWN

Bobby Hull's hockey career stretched from 1957 through 1980. The left winger was known as the "Golden Jet." Playing for the Chicago Black Hawks, he amazed reporters with his speed—28.3 miles per hour, 29.7 mph without the puck to slow him down. Hull's slapshot was timed at 118.3 miles per hour, almost 35 mph faster than the NHL average.

Hull and fellow Chicago wing Stan Mikita combined to change the face of hockey, all from a bit of pregame fun. The teammates fooled around with a stick that had warped, curving the blade. The angle created incredible spins on booming slapshots—so incredible that Hull took the warped blade into a game. Goalies who had always worried about guarding Hull now had a brand-new nightmare. Luckily for

Brett Hull, in action here, followed his famous father, Bobby Hull, into a career in hockey. Brett's dad led the NHL in goals seven times and scored 610 goals during 16 NHL seasons.

them, as players on other teams discovered the secret, the NHL passed rules on how curved a blade could be.

Bobby's son, Brett Hull, is a talented right winger who has been an NHL fixture since 1987. After leading the NHL in goals scored for three straight years (1989–1991), questions about being as good as his famous father lessened.

Many fans focus only on who scores, instead of on the winger who decoys ("dekes") a goalie out of position, opening up a scoring window for a teammate. But John Ogrodnick, a 14-season left winger with three different teams through 1992–1993, said, "My game was getting open in the holes, getting the puck, giving it to someone, getting away from my check, getting in the hole again, and waiting to get the puck back. My game was quickness, shot, give-and-go. My weakness was I wasn't a fighter, and I wasn't a stick-handler. I wasn't a guy who could dipsy-doodle out there [with fancy puck handling]."

Coaches don't always care about scoring, either. Right

winger Rick Middleton's 14-season NHL career began in 1974. Acquired by Boston from the Rangers after two seasons, Middleton scored a "hat trick" in his Bruins debut. His triple-goal game didn't make him an instant favorite with head coach Don Cherry, though. "He basically benched me for the rest of the year, because, as he said, I didn't know how to check my hat." (Middleton's coach was joking about how public places sometimes have supervised coatrooms where people may leave their hats and coats.) Middleton said his new coach wanted him playing a more defense-oriented game.

Can fame be passed from father to son? After Chicago retired Bobby Hull's number 9, the number almost appeared again. When son Brett Hull considered signing with the Black Hawks for the 1998–1999 season, Dad said he'd allow his offspring to wear the famed digit. The Hull-to-Hull handoff never happened, though, as Brett joined Dallas.

FIGHT OR FLIGHT

Coach Cherry isn't alone in his wishes. The NHL awards the "Frank J. Selke Trophy" to a forward who best excels in the defensive aspects of the game. Historically, wingers like Howe found that good winger defense means being willing to fight.

Yet hockey also recognizes "clean play" with the Lady Byng trophy. Anaheim winger and team captain Paul Kariya won that trophy for the 1995–1996 season. Kariya had once told reporters, "I like fighting—when everybody else does it. I don't want to participate in it."

But as Kariya gained fame as perhaps the best active player to shoot "off the pass" (right after touching the puck), defenses swarmed on him. During the 1997–1998 season, Kariya was cross-checked in the jaw, suffering a concussion.

No, hockey players don't knit their jerseys. However, because hockey began as an outdoor sport, their tops are still called "sweaters" by many fans.

He missed the last 28 games of the season. After three months on the disabled list, Kariya revised his earlier statement. "Maybe I've got to get my stick up a little bit and rack up some more penalty minutes," he said. "I've got to protect myself a little better."

From the left or right, wingers are not finding today's hockey to be kinder or gentler. Speed, strength, and smarts are the game plan not only for success but for survival.

CENTER OF IT ALL 5

In the beginning, a center might have earned the name from his position at center ice for a game's initial face-off. Today, the center's name seems to describe the position's importance. A center is at the center of every play: After all, a center's job is to travel the ice from end to end while leading a team's offense and defense.

If a hockey dictionary had an entry for "great center," the two-word definition would probably be "Wayne Gretzky." In the hockey world, he is known simply as "The Great One."

Gretzky's pro career began at age 18, when he signed an $875,000, four-year contract with the Indianapolis Pacers. Edmonton bought Gretzky's contract when the Pacers folded later that year, and he ended his first year with 51 goals and an MVP award. Since then, the player wearing number 99 has been saluted as a superb playmaker. Gretzky's fabled passes are matched by his finishing ability. A good center starts plays. Gretzky finishes them, too, making goals happen. Gretzky amassed 92 goals in 1981–1982, and 163 assists in 1985–1986; these are just two of his 60-plus league offensive records.

A sharing center who has been compared with Gretzky is Adam Oates. Oates powered Washington's drive to the 1997–1998 Stanley Cup finals. His odd NHL start came in June 1985, when he signed as an undrafted free agent with Detroit. "I was one of those later bloomers," Oates said. "My draft years, I was playing in the Northern Toronto

Wayne Gretzky holds numerous hockey records and has won a number of awards. Among them is the Hart Memorial Trophy as MVP in the NHL, which he first won at age 19 in 1980. Here New York Ranger Gretzky goes after the puck.

League and was a little small, a little slow, and I just didn't get the recognition. I think at that age, they [scouts and teams] have a tendency to go for the bigger kids and kids that are a little bit more heralded."

FORWARD THINKING

A center is also called a forward, but few of them take on the added role of a "power forward." Usually, a winger holds down the power forward spot. Phoenix Coyote center Jeremy Roenick is an exception.

Like the best "power forwards," Roenick camps close to the crease, absorbing bumps and crosschecks from defensemen to screen the goalie and tap in rebounds. Roenick and other power forwards are among the first in on a forecheck, hoping to produce a turnover by making contact with a retreating defenseman.

Another special class of centers, according to longtime Red Wings fan Steve Fortuna, is that of "pure scorers," players like Fedorov, Lemieux, and Gretzky. "They seldom take hits, and the best way to stop them is to knock them down," Fortuna said. "They are much rarer than power forwards. A team is lucky to get one!"

Some rival coaches feel that the way to stop a pure-scoring center is to assign him a "shadow," someone who can slow down the speedy point producer. A shadow's strategy isn't always physical.

New York Ranger Esa Tikkanen does more than play defense—he haunts pure scorers. Gretzky has called Tikkanen the best checker ever. Tikkanen is from Finland, and combines his native Finnish with English to tease and taunt foes in two languages. His teammates call the chatter on ice "Tikkanese." It's the same style of bad-boy defense that basketball's Dennis Rodman perfected. Once, Tikkanen's remark to famed center Mario Lemieux caused that Pittsburgh great to punch him. Tikkanen smiled about it later, innocently telling reporters, "I just asked him how his Mom was doing."

Center Mario Lemieux was a tough assignment for any defenseman. Lemieux's statistics were big, and so was he: At 6 feet 4 inches and 225 pounds, the longtime Penguins star had a long reach and bulk that sheltered the puck. Ice boss Scotty Bowman relied on Lemieux's play as he led Pittsburgh to its second Stanley Cup in a row.

BOWMAN'S BOYS

Bowman also won in Detroit with the flare of Sergei Fedorov. Fedorov was "center" in the Red Wings drive for a return to the Stanley Cup championship in 1997–1998. A Red Wing since 1990, Fedorov's scrappy play won him the Selke Trophy twice (1993–1994 and 1995–1996) as the league's best defensive forward. He capped the 1993–1994 season with the Hart Trophy, putting up MVP numbers of 56 goals and 64 assists.

Fedorov's fellow Red Wing center Steve Yzerman cranked out 155 points in 1988–1989, but his offense declined to 24 goals in 1997–1998 when Fedorov came on board. Coach Bowman told team captain Yzerman that there wasn't as much pressure to score, with Fedorov helping out. Bowman believed that "players enjoy not having to get all the goals . . . getting to lay off the numbers. They enjoy winning more."

Bowman should know, after working with so many great centers. Of those greats, Bowman calls Lemieux the best he ever coached. But hockey fans love to wonder: who was the best ever?

Some would vote for Howie Morenz, a balding center who never topped 165 pounds. Leading the Montreal Canadiens to three Stanley Cup wins, he became a giant of 1920s hockey. "When Howie skates full speed," a foe once said, "everyone else on the ice seems to be skating backward." Morenz played briefly for the Chicago Black Hawks in the 1934–1935 season but returned to the Canadiens for the 1936–1937 season. At the time Morenz played, his 270 career goals made a mammoth record.

Howie Morenz was a star center in the 1920s and early 1930s. As a Canadien, he was the leading scorer in the NHL in 1928 and 1931. He later played briefly for the Chicago Black Hawks and the New York Rangers, then returned to the Canadiens.

Sadly, his career, and life, ended too soon. Two Chicago players brutally body-checked him into the boards. With a skate caught in the wood, Morenz's leg was broken in four places. In the hospital some five weeks later, he suffered a fatal heart attack.

His 1937 funeral was held at the Montreal Forum, with his casket on center ice. The arena was packed with 10,000 fans, with 15,000 more outside in the cold Canadian night. A hockey legend was dead at age 34.

Although others have exceeded Morenz with statistics, today's centers face the same constant scrutiny he did. Consider Mark Messier, whose career in the NHL dates from 1979. In 1997–1998, he became the sixth player in league history to reach 1,000 career assists. Yet Messier said, "Individually, I don't think I've had the talent that a lot of the players have had," he said. "I've really learned to try to play inside a team concept. The true richness of the game comes from completely becoming selfless. Helping players learn that is kind of the exciting part of the game for me right now."

It's no small wonder that centers often become team captains. In attitude and action, they know where to center their efforts.

THE "D" MEN

6

The first defenseman to carve his name in the ice was Lester Patrick.

The pioneering Patrick inspired defensemen on defense. Before Patrick, both defenders would line up, one behind the other. Current defensemen who stand side by side can thank Patrick for the idea. The Canadian amazed hockey watchers in 1904 when he refused to play the expected, limited role of passing to a shooter soon after intercepting a puck. Instead, Patrick hustled the puck the entire length of the ice, ready to score himself.

Decades later, Boston hosted a 22-year-old wonder who completed the definition of defenseman that Patrick had started to write. Bobby Orr racked up 33 goals and 87 points in 1970. Never before had a defenseman led in these famed offensive departments.

Orr's biggest contribution in 1970 may have been scoring the game-winning goal against the St. Louis Blues to win the Stanley Cup. Coach Scotty Bowman's favored Blues fell in four straight to a Boston team that hadn't been champs since 1941. "They say Boston started rebuilding this year," Bowman said. "I don't believe that. I think they started rebuilding in 1948, the year Bobby Orr was born." Before he was through, Orr would be an eight-time winner of the James Norris Trophy, awarded each season to the league's top defenseman. Sadly, after six knee operations, Orr retired at age 30.

Despite Patrick and Orr, many current teams still expect defensemen to stick to defense. Along with their ability to use their sticks and bodies to dead-end shooters, defensemen have to pass. After all, what good is a player stealing the puck if he is unable to dish it off to a teammate? Being able to make the switch to offense, and get a scoring opportunity started, is what the best defensemen do.

Bobby Orr, shown here in action with the Boston Bruins, was both a top defenseman and a leading scorer.

WINNING AT THE SLOTS

Often, turning a game around begins for defensemen in the "slot." The two players in the slot serve as advance goalies, patrolling the space directly in front of the goal. The fight for the puck turns into a dance. Some defensemen favor the "poke check." They jab their stick, one-handed, at a foe's stick or the puck. This pushbroom motion is more sudden than the "stick lift," where a defenseman's stick lifts that of an opponent, causing a loose puck. Someone

The pile-up of players on the boards, battling for the puck, has a name borrowed from another sport. "Scrum" is a term from the game of rugby, describing how the huddle of both teams becomes a struggle for the ball. The word dates from 1885–1890.

with an octopus-wide reach can try the "sweep check." This move is something like swinging a butterfly net across the ice, hoping to sweep up the puck.

Backchecking is a more aggressive defense. When the other team comes to collect a puck, defensemen will use their backs to keep the offense in one place—away from the puck. Backchecking seems gentle compared with bodychecking. A defender's body becomes a shield to stop someone from grabbing the puck. If an opponent with possession can be trapped near the boards, a teammate may be able to swipe the puck.

Of course, the best checking among defensemen is the kind that doesn't draw a penalty. Charging, checking from behind, elbowing, holding, kneeing, tripping—these are some penalties whose names explain the crimes. Other no-nos are done with the stick: hooking, slashing, spearing, and high-sticking, when someone carrying his stick above the waist whacks another player.

Chris Pronger, who became St. Louis Blues team captain in 1997–1998, was asked by his coach to avoid the penalty box. "Emotions run high out there, but you can't get too caught up in it. You can't lose your focus on your job. You can't let them get the best of you out there and let guys get you off your game," he explained. Defensemen are

Ice hockey is a rough sport!

almost expected to be on-ice bullies. Expecting the worst might make opposing players treat defensemen aggressively, and revenge is tempting. But going too far could result in a penalty and a short-handed team. The best revenge is delayed revenge—a win. But best isn't always easy.

Pronger praises longtime Boston defensemen Ray Bourque as a role model at his position. Bourque broke the 1,000 career assists barrier in 1996–1997, becoming only the second defensemen in history to grab the honor. (After all, it's hard to rack up assists from the penalty box!) Bourque debuted with the Bruins as an 18-year-old in 1979, and became Rookie of the Year. Bourque bet on a future in hockey. He dropped out of school at age 15 to play full-time in a junior league.

> "I didn't have a bonus for goals, so why not set up the guys who needed them?"
>
> —Defenseman Doug Harvey, telling why scoring didn't pay. His attitude paid off, gaining 11 All-Star appearances in 17 years, entering the Hall of Fame in 1973.

Bruins general manager Harry Sinden says he didn't worry about Bourque's early defensive weaknesses. Bourque hadn't had a chance to practice defense "because he dominated the junior game. He had the puck all the time," Sinden said. "He didn't need to work hard on defense." Under Sinden, Bourque learned.

A NEW GAME PLAN

It takes courage to change, to do the unexpected, even what seems wrong. Scott Stevens, New Jersey Devils defenseman, had spent years defending against two attackers by going to one knee and stretching out the stick with one hand. Coach Jacques Lemaire showed Stevens that, though these moves might break up a play, following through with another play was tough. If Stevens got the puck on one knee, he had to stand and get both hands on the stick, ready to travel. All that took just enough time to lose the puck to an opponent.

"I really wasn't sure if I thought [staying up] was right," Stevens said, "but after awhile, I became very good at it. It's just practice,

"Changing on the fly" is the term for hockey substitutions in the middle of a play. Unlike other sports, subs may enter without a time-out being called. Done well, the changing looks like musical chairs on ice.

getting confidence in your stick and your positioning," he explained about the 2-on-1 breakout. "If you have [the stick out] there to start with, [the other team is] not going to try the pass. So sometimes you can try to dictate where the guy's going to put the puck by giving him [room] then taking it away."

The ability to keep learning, to keep changing, is one of the most important athletic abilities, an ability every game plan depends on.

SETTING GOALS

7

Although a net-minder isn't marked with multiple circles like the target bow-and-arrow shooters know, coaches do teach shooters seven targets that every goalie can be beaten with.

Shoot the puck between a goalie's legs, or under either arm. Aim for spots left or right of a goalie's shoulders, or beside either foot. Even the largest goalie can't block every inch of the exposed net in the area 4 feet high and 6 feet wide. Former goalie Emile Francis believed that a shot on the stick-hand side between the knee and ankle was toughest to handle.

Buffalo Sabres goalie Dominik Hasek caught the world's attention with his defense during the 1998 Olympics. Playing for his native Czechoslovakia, Hasek helped his homeland to a gold medal against a highly-favored American team stocked with NHL stars. In one game, Hasek even offered his head as a shield, purposely deflecting an oncoming shot with his helmet!

Hasek's brawn is matched by his brains. He's skilled at keeping track of the puck and of opposing team members. As 1997–1998 ended, he became the first goalie ever to win two straight Hart Trophy (MVP) awards. Combine that with a Lester B. Pearson award (as Outstanding Player), and a fourth Vezina Trophy (top goalkeeping) in five seasons, and it's clear that Hasek is the secret to Buffalo's success.

Buffalo Sabres goalie Dominik Hasek stretches in front of the goal to stop the puck in this April 23, 1998, Eastern Conference quarter-finals game. The Sabres beat the Flyers 4-1.

Hasek ranked near the top of NHL lists when it came to speedy reactions. Other goalies have won acclaim for different skills. Take St. Louis Blues goalie Grant Fuhr. He shines with his "catcher," using his mitt hand to snatch pucks like a hungry frog snatches flies. The left-handed Fuhr's snatches are the most confusing to other left-handed players.

"I find it tough to play against left-handed goalies," said Paul Kariya, left-handed left wing of the Mighty Ducks. "All the goalies are good, but guys like Grant Fuhr and Daren Puppa, who catch with their right hand, kind of screw you up a little bit." It's easier to get a goal past a mitt than a stick. When a lefty faces a right-handed goalie—whose mitt on the left hand—his natural swing usually sends the puck toward the mitt.

But stopping opponents from scoring won't mean a lot to a goalie who can't help his team get chances. A goalie who loses control of a blocked puck likely will face a bunch of second-chance shots. Getting a rebound back to your own team quickly and accurately is a job skill that all goalies need.

THE MASKED MAN

Jacques Plante of the Montreal Canadiens modernized the role of goalie by accident—his own! On November 1, 1959, Plante blocked a shot from New York Ranger Andy Bathgate, receiving a broken nose.

"His whole face was a bloody mess," teammate Maurice "Rocket" Richard said. "He went into the dressing room and told coach Toe Blake he wouldn't play any more if he couldn't wear the mask." Plante's coach wasn't pleased. No goalie wore a mask back then. How could any goalie see from behind a mask and get the job done?

"But there was nothing Blake could do," Richard said. Plante, a six-year veteran, felt entitled to demand special treatment—and the added incentive of a game on the line didn't hurt his cause. "He let Jacques finish the game with that big thing over his face." Plante's mask was a skin-colored plastic shell, far from the facial armor of current net-minders.

The newly masked man kept Montreal champions through 1960. For the 1961–1962 season, Plante captured the Hart Trophy, given to hockey's most valuable player. The mask probably helped him achieve his long, productive career: Plante played through the 1974–1975 season.

Today's mask-helmets are fashionable and practical. Mask designs that began as team logos have become part of a game of intimidation, with mon-

Would a goalie fit in a "bird cage?" That's what goalkeepers called the early models of helmets with wire face masks. Dave Dryden, a goalie, made his own in 1979, adapting an old fiberglass face mask with a soldering gun.

> In 1976 a Canadian junior league goalie's neck was slashed by an opponent's skate. His father invented the "crotch collar," to protect the area that the mask can't. The collar is made of ballistic nylon, the fabric that meatcutters wear for protection.

strous faces covering much of the goalie's humanity. But the designs protect his humanity, too. Over the years, parts of the head left exposed by the old helmets have been covered: The new designs protect ears, Adam's apples, and more. Other athletes took notice: Catchers for the Toronto Blue Jays were the first in the 1990s to introduce similar headgear to baseball.

The headgear of current goalies is different from that of their teammates, and so is their footwear. The blades on a goalie's skates (actually called "boots") are slightly wider, to aid in side-to-side movement, traction, and preventing pucks from sneaking through. The blades have a plastic shell, to reduce wear from puck contact.

ISOLATION ON ICE

A goalie's uniform is protective, but also isolating. Goalies are not allowed to be captain or alternate captain because games might take too long if slow-skating, overdressed goalies were the chosen players to chase down referees for protests. This isolation may explain why goalies traditionally have not been seen as masterminds in a team's game plan. When Emile Francis became coach of the New York Rangers in 1965, he was the first former goalie to get such a job in the NHL since 1927. Francis later took on the dual role of general manager of the Rangers.

During Francis's playing days and throughout the 1950s, teams expected one goalie to play full-time. As the NHL increased its number of games per year, teams became concerned about the health of their one goalie. In the early 1960s, teams began adding a second goalie to their rosters. Sharing the job between two players means that old career records such as Terry Sawchuk's (971 games played,

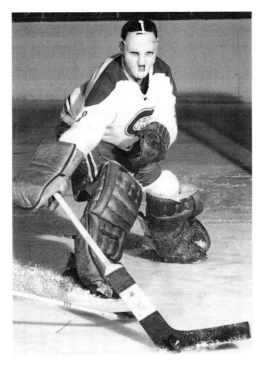

Protective equipment for a goalie has changed over the years, particularly the face mask. Contrast the 1950s equipment worn by Jacques Plante of the Canadiens (*left*) with the 1990s face mask and gloves worn by Bill Ranford when he was with the Capitals (*right*).

447 wins, 57,205 minutes, 103 shutouts) may be untouchable for to-day's goalies.

Goalies encountered more changes in their roles as the 1997–1998 season ended. NHL general managers started to worry about all the equipment goalies used. When Phil Esposito was general manager of the Tampa Bay Lightning, he talked about changes in the game since his own career. "When I fool around with the guys and I go on the ice and I try to shoot at the goalie, there isn't a lot of net you see," he said, "especially if a guy is six-foot tall or more. All of a sudden, the catching glove looks like a bushel. How are you supposed to miss that?"

A goalie's job, of course, is to stop goals. But league officials wondered: Would more offense—more goals scored—bring more fans? To see if that would happen, the net was moved an additional 2 feet from the end boards. If a goalie had more space to patrol, more points might

Why did some reporters
write that Detroit goalie
Chris Osgood's helmet
mask looks old-fashioned?
The Red Wings netminder
has no artwork on his
headpiece.

result. Even tougher was a rules change reducing the size of the "crease," the semicircle of protected space for the goalie to work from. The space would shrink by 2 feet on both sides of the goalposts.

Will all this make the game more fun for the fan? Certainly, the game will become more challenging for net-keepers. Mask innovator Plante described the pressure that goalies felt in his day—pressures that may not have changed so much.

"How would you like it if you were sitting in your office and you made one little mistake? Suddenly, a big red light went on behind you and 18,000 people jumped up and started screaming at you, calling you a bum and an imbecile. Then, they started throwing a lot of garbage at you. Well, that's what it's like when you play goal for a team in the NHL."

Goalkeepers' jobs aren't going to get easier. But new rules bringing new challenges are going to make for new game plans, better strategies, and better goalies than ever.

SEEKING STANLEY 8

While much of North America knows green grass and sunshine, two teams still remain on the ice. All NHL teams dream of June glory, of summer frost, a time to compete for the Stanley Cup.

The 1998 matchup looked good for the Red Wings—maybe too good. Detroit had more experience, more talent, and fewer injuries, the media reported. Newscasters pressured the defending champs to wrap up another Cup in four straight wins.

But a few reporters didn't believe Detroit was a "sure thing." After all, the team had struggled to advance in the playoffs against the Dallas Stars. Losing coach Ken Hitchcock didn't speak of how Detroit had played. Instead, he said, "The thing that is impressive is their resolve. They got pushed to the limit in this series. They know it, we know it, their players know it, and their coaches know it. But they responded. Champions do that," Hitchcock said. "If they continue to maintain focus they are going to be difficult. They learned that there is an awful high price to pay to win in the end. They know that price, and some of us are still learning."

Even Detroit coach Scotty Bowman was uncertain about his team's initial home ice advantage. "There's a lot of pressure in opening up a series at home," he said. "When you're at home, you've got more distractions, too, and you know the visiting team is going to be on a high."

So Bowman tried to focus his club by bragging about the *other* team, not his own. "They're a team that just got better and better," he told the media about the Capitals. Bowman didn't comment about the fact that the Capitals hadn't won a single game in Detroit in the past four years. Instead, he painted a gloomy picture for the Red Wings: "[This group of Capitals] is not the team that played during the season."

Team captain Steve Yzerman talked down his team, too, remembering how the first three rounds of the playoffs took six games each. "It seems like forever since the playoffs started. We haven't won anything yet," he said.

Modern communications equipment is essential to broadcasting a fast-paced game such as ice hockey. After the game, coaches and players may make use of the broadcast and updated stats to analyze the action.

A STRANGE HOMECOMING

For Washington's coach Ron Wilson, playing Detroit in Detroit for the Cup was a strange homecoming. His father, Larry Wilson, had been a winger for the Red Wings from 1949–1953. Wilson carried a trading card of his dad in uniform.

At home in Joe Louis Arena for Game 1, Red Wing Tomas Holmstrom tied up Washington's Adam Oates in front of the Washington net. Goalie Olaf Kolzig couldn't see well as Nicklas Lidstrom slapped it home.

"We talked throughout the playoffs of having people in front of the net, trying to screen, or be there for tips or rebounds," Lidstrom said. Holmstrom followed that game plan to perfection. Goalie Chris Osgood praised the way his team "kept the puck to the outside," limiting Washington to just 17 shots, and the Red Wings collected a series-opening 2–1 win.

At the 1998 Winter Olympics in Nagano, Japan, the first medals for women's ice hockey were awarded. Team USA brought home the gold. The whole team was pictured on a Wheaties box.

Offense exploded in Game 2. Twice Detroit fell behind by two goals, and the game went into overtime as Detroit slapped its way to 60 shots.

At 1:51 into the second period, Washington's Peter Bondra scored after Jeff Brown sent the puck from the Capitals' zone and brought it past the Detroit blue line. Was that icing? Detroit goalie Osgood thought so, ignoring Bondra's shot, which would be worthless when a penalty was called.

When a penalty was called—but no whistle blew. The video replay proved that a teammate's stick had touched the puck in the neutral zone, erasing any chance of icing. Mind-reading the officials shouldn't be part of any game plan, Osgood learned.

The Capitals almost put the win on ice with 9:52 left in the game. Esa Tikkanen's breakaway faked out Osgood again, caught off-stride and offering up an empty net. A near miss saved the fooled goalie, and the Red Wings. Kris Draper scored the game-winner in overtime, and Detroit took home a second win, 5–4.

After a quiet first-game workload, Red Wings goalie Chris Osgood had said , "I don't mind at all if they don't get any shots. That means they can't score." He must have been happy during Game 3.

A smothering defense kept the Capitals to just one first-period shot. "We played 16 or 17 minutes in our own end," moaned Craig Berube. "You can't score when you do that. We made it easy on them."

Although Washington got off 17 shots during the rest of the game, they didn't score until their final try. The Red Wings broke the 1–1 tie

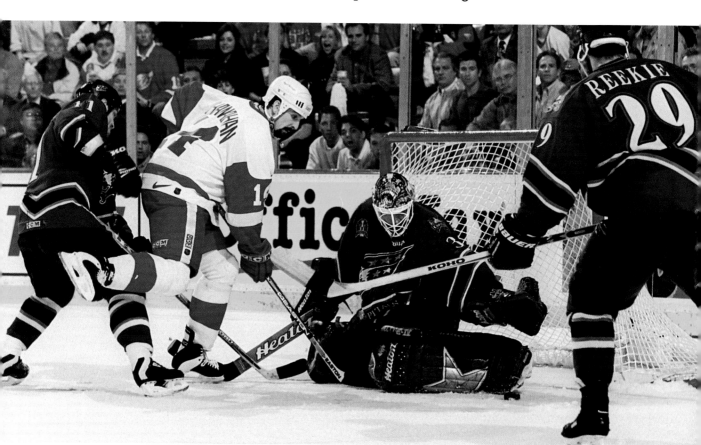

Game 2 in the 1998 Stanley Cup Finals went to overtime, where the Red Wings defeated the Capitals 5-4.

with 4:51 left in the game. Sergei Fedorov's shot, providing the 2–1 win, marked the first time since 1976 that the first three games of a Stanley Cup match had been decided by one goal.

SWEEPING AND WEEPING

It took more than one goal to win the fourth game, but the first goal remained the key to the title. Through the four rounds of postseason play, the Red Wings owned a 13–1 record after scoring first. After pulling ahead quickly, Detroit was free to use its famed left-wing lock defensive system to protect that lead.

Creating that offense was a shared job. Throughout the playoffs, every Red Wing had scored a point, even goalie Osgood—and the Red Wings took home their second Stanley Cup, winning in four straight, just like the media had predicted, just like the team must have secretly hoped, even while praising their foes the week before.

For the Red Wings, the sweep had special meaning: It was a way to salute their sidelined team members. When the smiling Konstantinov was helped from his wheelchair to his feet to wave to the crowd, the entire Detroit bench jumped to its feet, too.

With some two minutes still left in the game, the score at a comfortable 4–1, Coach Bowman had tried to calm his players. Chants of "Vlad-dy! Vlad-dy!" were echoing from the rafters. Bowman barked that no one had won anything yet, that nothing was over. Still, a few players were sure they saw a tear run down Bowman's cheek. Was this the man thought to have the hardest heart in hockey?

Finally, it was over. The Red Wings were officially champions, again. Even after the game was over, the Red Wings proved why they were champions.

Hockey's championship dates from 1893, when Lord Stanley of Preston, the governor-general of Canada, presented a silver cup to the top amateur team of his country. Since 1926 only NHL teams have battled for the trophy, a chance to celebrate being the champions of hockey and "hug the mug," as many players joke.

Team captain Steve Yzerman knew hockey tradition. To celebrate the championship in front of a wildly-cheering crowd, the captain was always chosen to skate a lap around the ring, waving the trophy to salute faithful fans. Then, the captain would pick a teammate to take the second lap, who would pass the trophy to the next local hero. Yzerman said his earliest thought was to take a lap, then share the glory with goalie Osgood. Teammate Brendan Shanahan asked, "What about Vladdy?"

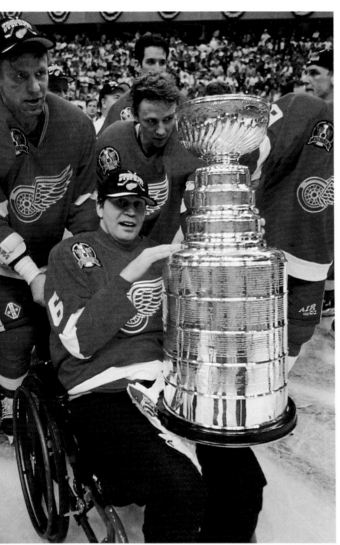

On June 16, 1998, at the end of a successful game plan, the Detroit Red Wings took victory laps by wheeling Konstantinov holding the Stanley Cup.

With that suggestion, Yzerman picked another Detroit hero to get the first moment with the Cup. The captain knew that, even in a wheelchair, Konstantinov continued to be an important member of the Red Wings. When team officials brought Konstantinov onto the ice to join in the celebration, Yzerman placed the trophy in his injured teammate's lap.

"When they brought Vladdy on the ice, it was automatic I was going to give the Cup to him," Yzerman said. "It was the appropriate thing to do."

All the Red Wings agreed. They took turns wheeling Konstantinov around the rink, with the Cup in his lap. Detroit proved that teamwork doesn't end when the game does—a championship game plan in any sport.

GLOSSARY

assist   when a goal is scored, the last two teammates to touch the puck are credited with assists. This statistic measures teamwork and unselfishness.

attack zone   the area between the opponent's goal and the nearest blue line. Also called *offensive zone*. The other end of the arena is the *defensive zone*.

backcheck   a maneuver by a forward skating back into the defensive zone to guard an attacking player from the other team.

blocker   the glove the goalie wears on the stick hand.

blue line   a line painted blue on each side of the center red line. Between the blue lines is the neutral zone. Used to determine offsides.

boarding   violently body-checking an opponent so he crashes into the boards. Results in a penalty.

boards   a wall about 4 feet high around the ice rink. Not made of boards, though it once was. Designed to keep the puck in play and protect fans.

body check   use of the hips or shoulders to bump an opponent in the area between his neck and knees. Legal only if opponent has possession of the puck, and if the check isn't too violent.

box   a defensive play used when a team is short-handed. Two defenders are positioned on either side of the goal and a bit forward. Another pair takes the same position closer to the blue line, forming a defensive box.

breakaway   a movement by an offensive player with the puck, with only the opposing goalie to face. All other opponents are behind.

breakout   a special play designed to get the puck out of a team's defensive zone so it can go on the attack.

butt-ending   using the top of the hockey stick to jab or attempt to jab an opponent.

catcher   the glove the goalie wears on the hand without the stick.

center   a forward who plays between the left and right wings

charging   an illegal body check, when a player takes three or more steps before making hard contact

changing on the fly   when a player leaves the ice and is replaced by a substitute from the bench while play continues.

clearing the puck   gaining control of the puck near a team's own goal and moving it away by passing or shooting

crease   the blue semicircle in front of the goal. No opponents may legally be in this area in advance of the puck.

cross checking   using the shaft of the hockey stick between both hands to check an opponent.

defensemen   usually two on the ice at any time. Defensemen try to keep play in their team's offensive zone. In the defensive zone, they try to keep the other team from scoring.

defensive zone   the area between a team's goal and the nearest blue line. The other end of the ice is the offensive zone.

deke   the first syllable of the word *decoy*. A decoy is something designed to mislead. In hockey, a deke may be a player moving right. The opponent follows, but the player quickly moves or passes left, surprising the unprepared opponent.

delay of game   stalling the progress of a game, as in intentionally knocking the net off its moorings or shooting a puck out of play.

directing the puck   making the puck go where you want it to by guiding it with the stick or your body.

dive   a maneuver in which a player tries to make an opponent get a penalty for hooking or tripping by falling to the ice on purpose so the opponent is blamed. The fallen player is said to "take a dive."

face-off   a method too start play in which an official drops a puck between two opponents who compete for control of it.

forecheck   a maneuver by a player in his offensive zone, trying to steal the puck from an opposing player who is in his defensive zone and create a turnover.

forward   the position of center and wing.

freezing the puck preventing the puck from moving by keeping it against the boards. Goalies are allowed to cover or "freeze the puck" in front of the goal line to keep the opponent from scoring. If there is no danger of scoring, the goalie will be called for delay of game.

goal the successful advance of the puck over the goal line and into the net, crediting the team with one point. A goal is also worth one point to the player scoring. A point is also awarded to each player assisting on the goal.

goaltender also called *goalie* or *goalkeeper*. The player stationed in the crease whose job is to keep the puck from crossing the goal line and entering the net.

head-butting using your head to hit an opponent.

heel of the stick the curve where the shaft and blade of a hockey stick meet.

high-sticking carrying the hockey stick above the shoulder and using it as a weapon against an opponent.

holding using the hands or arms on an opponent or opponent's equipment to impede his progress.

hooking using the stick as a hook to catch or detain an opponent. Also known as *water skiing*.

icing shooting the puck by a player from his side of the center red line over the opposing goal line while teams are at even strength. The penalty is a face-off back in the offending player's defensive zone. A team playing short-handed may "ice the puck" without penalty.

interference trespassing, by an offensive player in the crease. Also making bodily contact with the opposing goalie or with an opponent who does not have the puck.

linesmen one of the two types of on-ice officials. Responsible for calling offsides, icings, and conducting face-offs to resume play after a stoppage. Linesmen also report to the referee when they see too many players on the ice or a major penalty. Linesman cannot give penalties.

major an infraction for which a player must spend five minutes of actual playing time in the penalty box. The offending player's team must play shorthanded. Offenses resulting in a major include fighting or injuring an opponent.

minor   an infraction for which a player must spend two minutes of actual playing time in the penalty box. The offending player's team must play shorthanded unless scored upon before the penalty ends. Offenses resulting in a minor include holds, trips, hooks, and slashes.

misconduct   an infraction for which a player must spend ten minutes of actual playing time in the penalty box. The offending player's team may put a substitute on the ice right away. Offenses resulting in a basic misconduct include verbal abuse of an official and throwing a stick out-of-play. Game misconducts result in the player being removed for the rest of the game. They are given when the behavior is extreme, such as seriously injuring another player.

neutral zone   the area of the ice between the two blue lines.

offside   the crossing by an offensive player into the offensive zone before the puck, considered a violation. The teams have a face-off outside the blue line.

offside pass   a pass of the puck by a player from his defensive zone to a teammate who receives it across the center red line. Also called a two-line pass, because the puck crosses a blue and the center red line. The teams face-off where the puck was passed from.

one-timer   receiving the puck and shooting without stopping the puck.

penalty   punishment for breaking a rule, usually a time-out from the game during which the player's team is short a person. The PIM (penalty in minutes) varies. See *major*, *minor*, and *misconduct*.

penalty killing   keeping the opposing team from scoring even when short-handed because a player is being punished in the penalty box. Different plans must be used by a team that is outnumbered. Teams sometimes have a special penalty-killing unit of players.

point   either of the two areas in the offensive zone just inside the blue line and near the boards. Defensemen often station themselves here while their forwards play closer to the net or in the corners.

poke-check   trying to poke the puck away from an opponent with the hockey stick.

possession of the puck   control of the puck by the player who last made contact with it puck with body or equipment, intentionally or not.

power play   a situation in which one team has more players on the ice because the other team is playing short-handed. The team with more players on the ice has the power play.

red line   a line parallel to the goal lines and dividing the ice in half.

roughing   pushing, shoving, or hitting.

shoot-out   a device to avoid multiple overtimes in some international leagues. If a regulation game ending in a tie is still tied after a five-minute sudden victory overtime, five players from each team will shoot one-on-one against the opponent's goalie. Whichever team scores the most wins.

short-handed   having fewer players on the ice because of a penalty.

slashing   swinging the stick at an opponent, whether the opponent is hit or not. Results in a penalty.

slot   the area between the face-off circles down the center of the ice. The slot is the perfect place to try to score from. Moving defenders out of the area is called "clearing the slot."

smothering the puck   falling on the puck. It is legal only if done by a goalie. Accidental smothering carries no penalty.

sniper   a player, usually a forward, who has the ability to score many goals.

spearing   forcefully trying to poke an opponent with the blade of the stick while holding the hockey stick in both hands. The penalty is severe.

splitting the defense   a movement by the player with possession of the puck between two opponents.

stick-checking   using the stick to poke at an opponent's stick or the puck, while trying to gain possession of the puck.

sweep-checking   trying to gain possession of the puck by laying the stick down on the ice and using it in a sweeping motion.

turnover loss of possession of the puck by a team, with the other team gaining control.

two-line pass an offside pass that crosses two lines of the ice, a red and a blue.

wings two forwards, a left wing and a right wing, who stay on each side of the center. Wings try to help score on offense, and guard the opponent's wings when backchecking.

FOR MORE INFORMATION

Books

Duplacey, James. *Amazing Forwards* (Hockey Superstars). New York: Morrow Junior Books, 1996.

McFarlane, Brian. *Everything You've Always Wanted to Know About Hockey*. New York: Scribner's, 1971.

McFarlane, Brian. *Hockey for Kids: Heroes, Tips, and Facts*. New York: Morrow Junior Books, 1996.

Books for Older Readers

Davidson, John with John Steinbreder. *Hockey for Dummies*. Foster City, CA: IDG Books, 1997.

Fischler, Stan and Shirley Fischler. *Great Book of Hockey: More Than 100 Years of Fire on Ice*. Lincolnwood, IL: Publications International Ltd., 1997.

Hollander, Zander, ed. *Inside Sports Magazine Hockey*. Detroit: Visible Ink Press/Gale Research, 1998.

Hunter, Douglas. *A Breed Apart: An Illustrated History of Goaltending*. Chicago: Triumph Books, 1995.

Internet Resources

www.nhl.com
The league has its own web site, which offers games and other areas made especially for kids.

www.nhlpa.com

The NHL Players Association reveals salaries and more at this site.

www.hockeysfuture.com

Draft and scouting reports here give lots of inside information about current and future players.

www.hhof.com

The Hockey Hall of Fame in Toronto tells of its 300-plus honorees with this fine site.

www.thn.com

The Hockey News is a well-loved newspaper dedicated solely to hockey. Even players read it. You can, too, on-line!

INDEX